IRS Tax Helpline

The 7 Biggest Mistakes When Dealing With The IRS

Jules Marcel
1.855.240.1040   www.irstaxhelpline.com

Table of Contents

PAGE 2:   **Why You Need To Know the Facts**

PAGE 2:   **The 7 Biggest Mistakes When Dealing With the IRS**

PAGE 5:   **How To Get Rid of a Lien**

PAGE 6:   **IRS Levy Action**

PAGE 7:   **How Does the IRS Collect Money Owed by Taxpayers**

PAGE 7:   **Bank Levy**

PAGE 8:   **Understanding Wage Garnishments**

PAGE 9:   **Resolving Your Tax Problems**

PAGE 12:   **Penalties**

PAGE 13:   **Requests for Waivers and Penalty Abatements**

PAGE 14:   **Interest**

PAGE 14:   **Unfiled Tax Returns**

PAGE 16:   **How Can We Help You – Our 4 Step Plan to Resolving Your Tax Problem**

PAGE 18:   **The Services We Offer**

PAGE 20:   **IRS Forms 2848 & 8821**

PAGE 20:   **Legal Notice**

PAGE 24:   **Free Consultation**

Why You Need to Know the Facts!

The IRS is the most powerful collection agency on the planet. They are relentless in their efforts to collect tax dollars they believe are owed to the United States Treasury. The IRS has the power to take your property, place a wage garnishment, put a lien on your holdings and cause you much distress.

If you have a tax problem you need to understand what the IRS can do and what you need to do to protect yourself. By reading this e book you will obtain a stronger understanding of the IRS collection process. The e book will help you take tangible steps to resolve your tax problem with the IRS.

The 7 Biggest Mistakes When Dealing With the IRS

1. Procrastination and ignoring collection notices.
2. Not filing a tax return.
3. Believing the IRS when they say, "Don't worry, we'll fix of the problem."
4. Failing to hire proper representation fix your tax problem.
5. Failing to follow up on a tax Levy or Lien.
6. Allowing the IRS to file a tax return on your behalf.
7. Failing to remove a Federal Tax Lien from your record.

1. Procrastination and ignoring collection notices.
This is What Triggers the IRS Collections Process

The IRS collections process is long and complicated. There are two cases assigned to the collections division of the IRS.

1. The IRS collection process can be triggered by not filing required tax returns or,
2. By having unpaid tax debt.

The longer you wait (procrastinate) or completely ignore the collection notices sent by the IRS, the worse you problem becomes. For example, did you know that everyday your tax liability (amount you owe) goes up? That's EVERYDAY! The reason is that the IRS charges interest on the amount and that interest is compounded DAILY.

In addition, the IRS is charging you penalties. Penalties are for either 'Failure to File' and/or 'Failure to Pay'. Penalties are charged at a rate of up to 25% of your tax liability. Interest is also being charged on the penalties.

2.   Not Filing a Tax Return

Many taxpayers are guilty of not filing their taxes. This can be a serious problem.

Taxpayers must understand that 'it is NOT illegal to owe taxes, however, IT IS ILLEGAL NOT FILE YOUR TAXES.

The IRS receives what is called 'Wages and Income' from every source that you have earned money. That could be from your employer, interest you have earned or any other type of earned income.

If you haven't filed in several years, the IRS can and will do a 'Substitute File Return' (SFR). That means they file a return on your behalf. If they do and SFR, it is the worst kind of filing you can have. They file you as single, no dependants, no deductions and the highest tax rate. The outcome will be that you will owe a larger amount of tax as compared if you filed on your own.

The good news is you can have your SFR's amended and bring down your tax liability.

The bottom line is that you must file or amend all back taxes as quickly as possible. Do not ignore or procrastinate.

> THE GOOD NEWS IS YOU CAN HAVE YOUR SFR's AMENDED AND BRING DOWN YOUR TAX LIABILITIES

3. Believing the IRS when they say, "Don't worry, we'll fix of the problem."

Many taxpayer believe that if they call the IRS they can fix their tax problem. The truth is twofold. Yes you can call the IRS on your own. And NO they will not help you in your best interest.

The IRS Agents are usually trained on one or two areas of tax laws. In addition, the tax laws are quite complex and detailed. I have never met or talked to an IRS Agent who knows all the rules and laws.

Therefore when you try to speak to an Agent one of several things can happen;
1. You are on hold for a minimum of 15 to 20 minutes before you even get to speak with an Agent.
2. You speak with an Agent who doesn't know the correct rules/laws.
3. You get transferred to someone else who may or may not know the rules/laws.
4. If you get transferred, you will another 15 to 20 minute wait on hold.
5. You explain your situation to the Agent but don't have all the facts or documents needed during the call and have to call back again and go through the same process.
6. You get to speak to an Agent who is able to help you. HOWEVER, the help they give you will NOT be to your best interest. The Agents are trained and told in their manual to not have to provide the taxpayer with their best options unless the taxpayer asks for it. The IRS wants their money as quickly as possible.

7. The Agent will set you up on a monthly 'Installment Agreement'. Most taxpayers feel relieved to have that set up. However, the monthly amount requested by the Agent will not be the best or least amount as required by their rules. It will usually be much higher. Taxpayers don't know that they can request a different amount. <u>Do not simply accept the offer unless you know you can pay it every month and not default later.</u>

The facts are that as a taxpayer you have legal rights and the IRS is not obligated to tell them to you.

4. Failing to hire proper representation fix your tax problem.

If you are facing the possibility of an IRS audit or past due tax collection(s), we are ready to help you correct your problems. Our experienced CPA's are ready to provide the expert counsel and representation needed to get you through your particular IRS issue as quickly and painlessly as possible.

The IRS will only recognize a legally authorized representative after a power of attorney has been properly executed. The IRS has Forms 2848 and 8821 entitled Power of Attorney and Declaration of Representative. The power of attorney will stay in effect until it is revoked or until another Form is received without electing to keep the existing power of attorney on file. The power of attorney should be revoked by the taxpayer or withdrawn by the representative at the end of the engagement (See page 18 for a copy).

5. Failing to follow up on a tax Levy or Lien.

How to Stop the IRS Collections Process!

Enforced collections methods can be stopped by showing inability to repay or severe hardship or negotiate an alternative payment arrangement on your behalf.

6. Allowing the IRS to file a tax return on your behalf.

As we stated above, the IRS can and will file a 'Substitute File Return' (SFR) if you neglect to file. This is the worst possible type of filing you can have next to not filing at all. If you discover the IRS has an SFR filed on your behalf, you will want to have that SFR year or years amended as quickly as possible.

7. Failing to remove a Federal Tax Lien from your record.

Understanding Liens and Levies

The IRS has the power to attach all of your property and any property that you acquire in the future (Lien). If after protecting the government's interest, you cannot or will not fully pay the debt, the IRS has the power to seize

your assets (Levy). If you face this situation, I cannot fathom why you would want to face the full force of the United States Government without being properly represented.

A federal tax lien is the government's legal claim against your property when you neglect or fail to pay a tax debt. The lien protects the government's interest in all your property, including real estate, personal property and financial assets.

The heart of the Notice of Federal Tax Lien, IRC 6321 & IRC 6322 are as follows:

If any person liable to pay any tax neglects or refuses to pay the same after demand, the amount (including any interest, additional amount, addition to tax, or assessable penalty, together with any costs that may accrue in addition thereto) shall be a lien in favor of the United States upon all property and rights to property, whether real or personal, belonging to such person.

Internal Revenue Code section 6322 provides:
Sec. 6322. PERIOD OF Tax Lien
Unless another date is specifically fixed by law, the lien imposed by section 6321shall arise at the time the assessment is made and shall continue until the liability for the amount so assessed (or a judgment against the taxpayer arising out of such liability) is satisfied or becomes unenforceable by reason of lapse of time.

The IRS files a public document, the **Notice of Federal Tax Lien**, to alert creditors that the government has a legal right to your property. The filing of the Notice of Federal Tax Lien is the formalized process of notifying the rest of the world that you owe taxes. Please understand, the actual lien arose, when the IRS assessed the taxes to you. The IRS had to do nothing more than make a tax assessment. Unless you pay in full at the time of the assessment, the IRS has a tax lien against your property. This concept is referred to as a "silent lien".

The act of filing the Notice of Federal tax lien is purely to protect the Government's position and right of priority. The "silent lien" will attach to your personal property immediately after the IRS assesses a tax to you. The lien attaches to real estate when the IRS files the Notice of Federal Tax Lien in the county in which you own the real estate.

How to Get Rid of a Lien

Paying your tax debt - in full - is the best way to get rid of a federal tax lien. The IRS releases your lien within 30 days after you have paid your tax debt.

Options: When conditions are in the best interest of both the government and the taxpayer, other options for reducing the impact of a lien exist.

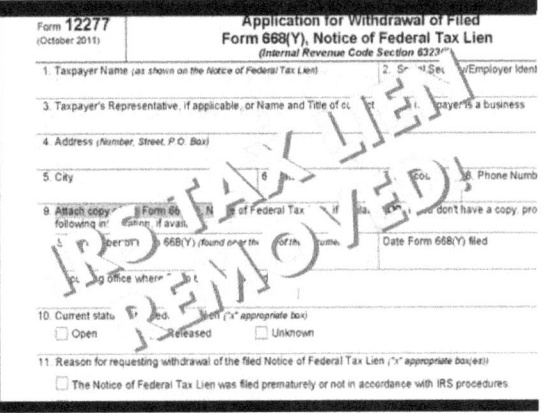

- **Discharge of property** — Allows property to be sold free of the lien.
- **Subordination** — Does not remove the lien, but allows other creditors to move ahead of the IRS, which may make it easier to get a loan or mortgage.
- **Withdrawal** — Removes the public notice and assures that the IRS is not competing with other creditors for your property. A withdrawal of a Federal Tax Lien is not the same as a release of the Federal Tax Lien.

There are 3 ways to obtain a release of a Federal Tax Lien:
- The amount assessed plus interest is paid
- The amount assessed becomes legally unenforceable by reason of lapse of time
- A bond is furnished and sufficient in amount to secure the payment of the amount assessed plus interest.

That is it, 3 ways to obtain a release of the Federal Tax Lien. I have had this conversation with many clients. Countless clients are being sold the services of a competing firm that is telling the client, "Don't worry, we can get rid of the tax lien". This is my answer. There are only 3 ways to obtain a release of a federal tax lien.

IRS Levy Action

The Internal Revenue Code empowers the IRS to enforce collections upon a taxpayer's property or rights to property. The IRS can enforce collections against a taxpayer's salary and wages, bank accounts, or other money that is owed to the taxpayer. If the IRS seizes your property and or garnishes your wages you may be placed into an economic hardship. An IRS enforced collections action can render you unable to pay critical business and personal expenses.

The IRS seizes property every day. Seizure actions are very easy for the IRS to accomplish. Many enforced collections actions are handled thru the Automated Collections Systems. The IRS wanted your attention, and now they have it.

The consequences upon you and your family are immediate, and many times devastating. Without your payroll check, or without the money you had saved in your bank account, you may not be able to cover your essential bills.

If you do not pay your taxes or setup a payment arrangement, the IRS may seize and sell your property. The IRS can levy any type of real or personal property that you own or have an interest in. For instance,
- The IRS can seize and sell all property that you hold (such as your car or house), or
- The IRS can levy property that is yours but is held by someone else (such as your paycheck, retirement accounts (401K or IRA), dividends, bank accounts, licenses, rental income, accounts receivables, the cash loan value of your life insurance, or commissions).

The IRS will levy, but levies are a form of enforced collections the IRS must meet three requirements to issue a levy:
- The IRS has assessed the tax and sent you a *Notice and Demand for Payment;*
- You did not pay the tax or setup an installment arrangement; and The IRS will send you a Letter 1058. This is your *Final Notice of Intent to Levy and Notice of Your Right to A Hearing* (levy notice) at least 30 days before the levy.
- The IRS may give you this notice in person, leave it at your home or your usual place of business, or send it to your last known address by certified or registered mail.

How does the IRS collect money owed by tax payers?

You either pay the IRS willingly or the IRS will use enforced collections methods. If you do not pay your back taxes voluntarily, the IRS will lien, levy, place a wage garnishment and seize assets to enforce collections.

Bank Levy

What is an IRS bank Levy? How does an IRS bank Levy work? What can you do about an IRS bank Levy?

An IRS bank levy is an enforced collection action where a taxpayer's bank account is seized.

When a bank levy is imposed, the IRS freezes the taxpayer's bank account for 21 days. In the process, the taxpayer cannot access his funds nor withdraw money (except when the account balance is greater than the tax liability). The taxpayer will not be able to pay using a debit card. The debit card will not be honored. **If the taxpayer has outstanding checks before the levy was placed, these checks will not clear.** After the 21- day period, the bank is expected to give either the total amount available in the bank account, or to remit full payment to the IRS from the taxpayer's account.

A levy is the LEGAL TAKING (seizure) of your PERSONAL PROPERTY BY THE IRS to *satisfy your tax debt*

How does an IRS bank levy get lifted or released? The IRS allows the taxpayer 21 days to "fix" their tax problem before the bank remits the funds. The IRS allows a taxpayer to contact the IRS after a bank account is levied and work out the problem. The IRS will release a bank levy if the taxpayer can show a hardship. Has the IRS bank levy caused the taxpayer a hardship? Ways to show a hardship are an eviction notice, a foreclosure notice, a utility disconnection notice, or a grave medical concern. The IRS will release a bank levy if the IRS has made an error.

Wage Garnishment

A wage levy or wage garnishment is the legal way the IRS can collect your tax liability. They can force you into paying your debt. The IRS will contact your current employer and send them a notice of wage levy. Your employer will then take a portion of your pay and send it to the IRS (up to 80% of your gross wages) and then you get what is left. Can you live on what the IRS will leave you?

Can a garnishment be stopped even after the IRS has started to garnish my wages?

Yes! A wage garnishment can be stopped. The garnishment can be stopped, even after the IRS has started to garnish your paycheck. The IRS would prefer you to make some other form of payment arrangement rather than to enforce a garnishment.

Some options can be to:
- Pay the IRS in full. Enter into an installment agreement (This is the most common way to stop a levy.)
- File for an offer in compromise. If you cannot at any point in the future fully pay the IRS debt, an offer in compromise maybe the best way to resolve your problem.
- The IRS has the power to grant a Currently Not Collectible status. This allows the taxpayer time to financially recover. The IRS will not seek collections while a taxpayer's account is Not Collectible.
- File bankruptcy. This action will cease all IRS collections actions. Many taxpayers come into our offices financially devastated. This may be their only recourse.
- Change employers or quit your job. You don't get out of a hole by digging it deeper. Employment and a good job are hard to come by these days. I would never advocate this approach to dealing with your IRS problem. I don't like to run from problems, I like to deal with problems head on.
- The most common methods to stop a levy are to enter into an installment agreement, pay in full or file for an offer in compromise.

How much of my wages can the IRS take?

The IRS has a chart that shows your employer what to deduct. The chart shows exactly how much they can take from you. The IRS's goal is to collect all monies owed to them in the fastest way possible. They don't care if they leave you enough money to live on. Their chart uses the "national average" of required amounts to live and if your bills are higher than the average, you will be left with an amount not high enough to pay your bills. We have seen the IRS take 80% of taxpayer's paycheck, until the taxpayer has fully repaid the tax debt.

What kinds of wages can the IRS take?

The IRS can seize your salary, commissions and bonuses. The IRS can seize other types of income as well. They can seize retirement money and pension earnings, rental income and dividend income. If you do not have any of those they will likely try to seize any other property you have, like your bank accounts and other property you own.

How can I avoid the IRS from garnishing my wages and property?

The best way to avoid any levy action is to prepare and file all required tax filings and pay all taxes owed to the IRS. If you cannot afford to pay the IRS you must propose another form of payment arrangement to ensure that you pay back your taxes. The IRS has some flexibility and they have many methods available for those taxpayers that cannot afford their taxes. The repayment method you pick depends upon your financial and tax situation.

How can IRS Tax Helpline help you with an IRS wage garnishment?

Tax Resolution Helpline can help more than most people realize. We routinely obtain wage levy releases for our clients. Normally, a release of levy takes 2-5 business days. Even if the levy has already begun, contact us immediately, we can still obtain a wage levy release. To obtain a release of levy a tax payer must propose a collection alternative. The IRS has many programs and options available for you. Most likely, you will need a professional to analyze your financial and tax situation to determine the collection alternative that best suits your situation. You may not have the knowledge and experience to negotiate on your behalf as well as we can. You cannot afford to wait. The longer you wait the more of your income or property the IRS can take. If you hire us today, within 2-5 business days, we can obtain a wage levy release and begin the work needed to get you back into good standing with the IRS.

Resolving Your Tax Problems/Collection Alternatives

As stated prior, the IRS is the world's most powerful collection agency and they are ruthless in their efforts. If you find yourself facing enforced collection activity from the IRS

IRS Compromise Help
Walking you through the entire process.

such as a tax lien, bank levy, wage garnishment or asset seizure and want it released or stopped you need to propose to the IRS an alternative to those enforced collections actions. If you cannot pay in full you will not face enforced collection activities from the IRS if you have in place an alternative for the service to collect such as an installment agreement.

Proposed Collection Alternatives to Enforced Collections

Revenue Agents within the IRS work in exam, collections and compliance. So if you are facing enforced collection activity from the IRS you will be dealing with a Revenue Officer. There are several collection alternatives that could be proposed to stop enforced collection activity. The following are just a few alternatives to enforced collection:

1. Full Payment
2. Installment Agreement
   - a. Streamlined Installment Agreement
   - b. Non-streamlined Installment Agreement
   - c. Partial Pay Installment Agreement
3. Offer in Compromise
4. Declared as Currently Not Collectable

(1) Full Payment with in 60 or 120 Day Agreements

An extension of time to pay is limited to 60 days. An extension of 60 days or less is not considered an installment agreement.

(2) Installment Agreement (IA)

An installment agreement is in essence a payment plan. If you can't afford to pay off your tax debt all at once the IRS may agree to let you pay it off in monthly installments. If the IRS accepts your payment plan all other collection activities will stop immediately. A complete financial statement, Form 433, is usually only required for non-streamlined installment agreements, partial pay installment agreements or offer in comprises.

All installment agreements are subject to a user fee. User fees for installment agreements are as follows:
1. $105 – non-direct installment agreements (Not set up on automatic deduction from your bank account)
2. $52 – direct debit installment agreements (Set up on automatic deduction from your bank account)
3. $45 – reinstatements
4. $43 – new agreements for taxpayers with income at or below certain U.S. Department of Health and Human Services poverty guidelines

Guaranteed Installment Agreement

IRC 6159(c) requires the IRS to accept the taxpayer's proposal of an IA if the following conditions are met:
- The taxpayer is an individual and owes an income tax liability with an aggregate unpaid balance of assessment amount of $10,000 or less
- During the preceding five taxable years, the taxpayer (including their spouse if the requested IA is for a jointly filed return, has not failed to file or to pay income taxes, nor entered an IA for payment of taxes)
- The IA provides for full payment of the liability within 3 years
- The taxpayer agrees to continue to comply with the tax laws and the terms of the agreement for the period (up to 3 years) then agreement is in place
- A Guaranteed Installment Agreement must be allowed even if it is determined the taxpayer is trying to delay collections

Streamline Agreement (SIA)

The IRS has raised the threshold for using an installment agreement without having to supply the IRS with a financial statement from $25,000 to $50,000. This means that taxpayers who owe up to $50,000 in back taxes may enter into a streamlined agreement with the IRS that stretches the payment out over a series of months or years. The IRS also has raised the maximum term for streamlined installment agreements to 72 months from the preexisting 60-month maximum.

"A Note of caution: Penalties and Interest Will Continue To Accrue on Your Tax Liability

A strategy I have used from time to time when a client owes greater than $50,000 and doesn't want to disclose or prepare a collection information statement is to make a partial payment. The partial payment is used to bring the balance below $50,000 to then qualify for a streamlined installment agreement.

Non-Streamline Installment Agreement (NSIA) or Regular Installment Agreement

NSIA is considered when the taxpayer cannot qualify for a Streamlined Installment Agreement. A complete financial statement must be completed to determine the monthly payment amount(s). The tax plus all accruals must be paid in full within the CSED.

Partial Pay Installment Agreement (PPIA): If full payment cannot be secured by the CSED and the taxpayer has requested to make payments or has some ability to pay, a PPIA should be considered. PPIA's requires that equity in assets be addressed; taxpayers are required to use equity in assets to pay liabilities; however; complete utilization of equity is not always required as a condition of a PPIA. PPIA's require a Collection Information Statement and management review. All PPIA's are non-streamlined IA's; therefore require lien filing. The CSED is not extended by waiver. The American Jobs Creation Act of 2004 requires PPIA's be reviewed every two years. The review is conducted by the Centralized Case Processing organization.

(3)Offer-In-Compromise (OIC):

An offer in compromise allows you to settle your tax debt for less than the full amount owed. It may be a legitimate option if you can't pay your full tax liability or doing so would create a financial hardship. The IRS will consider your equity in assets and your ability to pay by analysis of your income and expenses. The IRS will generally accept an offer in compromise when the amount offered represents the most they can expect to collect within a reasonable period of time. The service refers to this amount as the full collection potential.

An **offer in compromise** is where you make a deal with the government

THE PROCEDURES:

Lump Sum: Submit an initial payment of 20 percent of the total offer amount with your application. Then pay the remaining balance of the offer in 5 or fewer payments after receiving written acceptance of your offer from the IRS.

Periodic Payment: Submit your initial payment with your application. Continue to pay the remaining balance in monthly installments while the IRS considers your offer. If accepted, continue to pay monthly until it is paid in full. While your offer is being processed by the IRS:

- Your non-refundable payments and fees will be applied to your tax liability (you may designate payments to a specific tax year and tax debt):

- Other collection activities are suspended!
- The collection statute expiration date is extended
- A notice of federal tax lien may be filed

What happens if your offer is accepted?
- You must meet all the offer terms listed in section 8 of Form 656 including filing all required tax returns and making all payments;
- Any refunds due within the calendar year in which your offer is accepted will be applied to your tax debt;
- Federal tax liens are not released until your offer terms are satisfied

What happens if your offer is rejected?
If your offer is rejected you can fight on. You may appeal a rejection within 30 days using Form 13711 Request for Appeal of Offer in Compromise.

(4) Declared Currently Not Collectible (CNC):

The IRS can declare a taxpayer as "currently not collectible" which means the taxpayer has no ability to pay his or her tax debts. The IRS requires proof that the taxpayer does not have the ability to repay. This proof is usually done by submitting IRS Form 433-F. Once the IRS establishes the taxpayer as currently not collectable it must stop all collection activities such as bank levies and wage garnishments. The service will continue to mail annual statements of the amount owed but it is not a bill. This is because while in the CNC status the 10 year collection statute continues to run.

Collection Statue Expiration Date (CSED):

Internal Revenue Code section 6502 provides that the length of the period for collection after assessment of a tax liability is 10 years. The collection statute expiration ends the government's right to pursue collection of a liability. As in most areas of taxation there are always exceptions.

Penalties

Penalty for Failure to Timely File Your Return: If a taxpayer is required to file an income or excise tax return and fails to timely do so, a late filing penalty may be assessed. The penalty is 5% of the amount of unpaid tax per month the return is late, up to a maximum of 25%. A minimum penalty of $135 may apply for late filing of an income tax return.

Penalty for Failure to Timely Pay Tax: If a taxpayer is required to pay an amount shown on his return, but the taxpayer fails to pay such amount (even if the reason of nonpayment is a bounced check), there is a penalty of 0.5% of the amount of unpaid tax per month the return is late up to a maximum of 25%.

Penalty for Failure to Timely Pay After Issuance of Notice: If a taxpayer fails to pay a tax or other amount required to be shown on a return and the amount is not shown on the return, the taxpayer may be liable for a penalty equal to 0.5 percent per month of such amount, for each month during which the failure continues, if the amount is not paid within 21 calendar days after the date of an IRS notice demanding the payment.

If both the failure to file and the failure to pay penalties apply during the same month, then the failure to file penalty is reduced by 0.5% each month.

The 25% cap above applies to the 5% late filing penalty and the 0.5% late payment penalty together. The late filing penalty may be waived or abated on showing of reasonable cause for failure. The failure to file penalty starts to accrue interest from the date the return was due, whereas the failure to pay and failure to show penalties begin accruing interest from the date of notice and demand.

Virtually every tax payer that I have represented wants to know, can the IRS charge me that big of a penalty? The answer is… YES and they do.

REDUCE PENALTIES AND INTEREST

Requests for Waivers and Penalty Abatements

1. Waivers are sometimes granted by legislation, regulation, or administrative pronouncements to provide relief from estimated tax penalties created by the retroactive application of a change in statute or Service position.

2. If the taxpayer establishes that the waiver criteria are met, take the necessary action to suppress or adjust the penalty as appropriate.

3. When a determination is made to cancel an estimated tax penalty because the individual is entitled to a waiver, the appropriate Penalty Reason Code must be entered either on the case file or the input document for entry to the Master File via the appropriate data entry method.

Bankruptcy

Income tax debts may be eligible for discharge under Chapter 7 or Chapter 13 of the Bankruptcy Code. Filing for bankruptcy is one of five ways to get out of tax debt, but you should consider bankruptcy only if you meet the requirements for discharging your taxes.

Chapter 7 provides for full discharge of allowable debts. Chapter 13 provides a payment plan to repay some debts, with the remainder of debts discharged. Under the new bankruptcy laws, tax debts are treated the same way in both Chapter 7 and Chapter 13 petitions. Not all tax debts are capable of being discharged in bankruptcy. The bankruptcy petitioner must have tax debts that meet five criteria for discharge.

Tax debts are associated with a particular tax return and tax year. The bankruptcy law lays out specific criteria for how old a tax debt should be.

Five Rules to Discharge Tax Debts: If the income tax debt meets all five of these rules, then the tax debt is dischargeable in Chapter 7 and Chapter 13 bankruptcy petitions.

1. The due date for filing a tax return is at least three years ago.

2. The tax return was filed at least two years ago.
3. The tax assessment is at least 240 days old.
4. The tax return was not fraudulent.
5. The taxpayer is not guilty of tax evasion.

Abatement of Penalties

Abatement Definition: a reduction in or waiver of a tax or other debt. Tax, interest, and penalty abatements are typically granted through special tax relief programs or as the result of a valid protest action by a taxpayer in the proper and legal format.

Just about every client I have ever represented has asked me "Can you get rid of the penalties?" The short answer is maybe. The long answer is it depends.

The question is do you have a reason that might allow the IRS to abate the penalty? It is my experience that you have a much better chance of getting a penalty abated if, this is your first penalty charged in the last 3 years, you have a reasonable cause and you have paid the base tax in full.

Interest

Interest is typically added to any tax unpaid from the time that the payment of tax was due to the date of payment. Interest rates are mandated and voted on by Congress and assessed by the IRS every three months. Currently, the IRS interest rate for underpayments of tax is **3% per year.** The interest is calculated for **each day your balance due** is not paid in full. Interest is assessed on the unpaid amount of tax plus any late filing or late payment penalties.

It is never too late to file your tax returns.

Un-filed Tax Returns

If you have not filed a tax return in a while, you may be wondering what options you have. It is generally in your best interest to file those back tax returns as soon as possible. If you need to file a prior tax year or even multiple years of tax returns, you want to ensure that the return is as accurate as possible. There are many reasons accuracy is important. Penalties and interest accrue from the base tax owed is one such reason. Another reason would be the possible implications from a state agency.

The IRS and most states exchange information. Also most states income taxes are based off of some deviation of your adjusted gross income from your federal income tax return. If your federal Adjusted Gross Income (AGI) is artificially high due to not taking all allowable deductions it will result not only in a higher federal income tax liability but also a higher state income tax liability.

When you fail to act before the IRS does, they will file a Substitute For Return (SFR) for you. When the IRS files an SFR for you it is their best guess. The IRS will typically file the return in the best interest of the United States government. This means they will file it as you were single or married filing separately with no deductions, credits, or expenses. The service will then tack on a variety of penalties and then assess interest.

This whole process is done to have the tax assessed. Once the tax is assessed the IRS can then use their steam roller of a system to collect.

Filing an unfiled tax return or even multiple years is not as big of a deal as you may believe. Even if you cannot pay the taxes that are owed with the return it may still not be the problem you made it out to be. It is a big deal if you keep waiting longer and longer to file your back return(s) because the consequences may get worse. One thing you need to know is the sooner you file your taxes the better off things are going to be.

No matter how you look at it the longer you wait the harsher the consequences may end up. You might be surprised to learn that filing back taxes may be the simplest way to get out of your tax problems. You do however need to protect yourself and have a plan.

I would recommend the following 5 steps:
1. The first step is to gather all of your information for each year you failed to file a tax return. Research thoroughly any missing information to be sure the return you file is correct. Do you have your W-2's, 1099's and mortgage interest statements? Many taxpayers with unfiled back tax returns have lost their tax records. You may contact the IRS to request a wage and income transcript. This transcript will give you the wage and income information you're missing. If you were self employed you may need to work with an accountant to help recreate an accounting or determine estimates for you.
2. The second step is filing your past due IRS returns. The question needs to be asked whether to file your tax returns yourself or hire a professional. If you decide to do it yourself be sure to use a reliable tax software. You should also plan on spending two to three hours on each year.
3. Protect your refunds. You need to know there are strict time limits for statute of refunds,   audits and collections. You should also know that if you owe taxes for other years, the refunds may be taken to offset those other debts.
4. Deal with the tax debt that is owed. You should have a plan for how you will pay off your tax debts. You will need a plan to protect yourself from IRS assessments, levies, liens and seizures. Your plan could be as simple as setting up a payment plan or writing a check for the full amount. Regardless of your situation you need a plan because ignoring the IRS can get you in trouble fast.
5. Plan ahead. If you found yourself owing in past years, you should do some tax planning for the current year. You should adjust the withholding in your paycheck by completing a new W-4 for your company's payroll department. If you make estimated tax payments they should be adjusted to fulfill your tax liability.

Criminal

One common question I hear often is can I go to jail because of my tax problems?
Yes, however only under extreme conditions. The IRS can send you to prison! Most of the cases that I read the sentences are 40 plus months in a federal prison. So yes, if you haven't filed or if you have misrepresented your income on the tax return you filed, I think you could be in a lot of trouble!

The government has certain conditions that it must prove, what you don't want to do is make any statement or perform any action that harms any possible defense to the conditions!

If the threat of a criminal charge is present, seek qualified representation immediately before you discuss your case with the IRS. The only rights you have are the ones you assert. Assert your right to be represented!

But don't be too concerned because the Internal Revenue Service Criminal Investigation Unit is severely understaffed. It faces such strict procedures that in practice only the most egregious tax crimes are referred to the Justice Department for prosecution

What does the government need to prove to establish a crime?
Tax evasion is a violation of 26 U.S.C. Section 7201. The government must prove beyond a reasonable doubt the following:
1. The existence of a tax deficiency;
2. An affirmative act constituting an evasion, or an attempted evasion, of the tax; and
3. Willfulness.

Any person who willfully attempts in any manner to evade or defeat any tax imposed by this title or the payment thereof shall, in addition to penalties provided by law, be guilty of a felony and, upon conviction thereof, shall be fined not more than $100,000 ($500,000 in the case of a corporation), or imprisoned not more than 5 years, or both, together with the costs of prosecution. The Department of Justice will often consider other charges as alternatives or supplements to the charge of tax evasion such as:
- Conspiring to defraud the United States, 18 U.S.C. Section 371
- Filing false returns, 26 U.S.C. Section 7206
- Endeavoring to obstruct the IRS Section 7212

How Can We Help You, Right Now!

If you are facing the possibility of an IRS audit or owe back taxes or are in collections, the IRS Tax Helpline stands ready to help you. Our experienced CPA's and EA's are ready to provide the expert counsel and representation needed to get you through your particular IRS issue as quickly and painlessly as possible. Our staff of CPA's and Enrolled Agents (EA's) has a proven track record of helping people resolve their tax problems.

Our Firm's Approach and What You Can Expect

Enjoy Life Again

Let Us Help You Solve Your
IRS Problem Today.

Our 4-Step Plan to Solving Your Tax Problems:

1. We will discuss your tax problem and analyze it in detail.

   a. We strongly believe that it is critical that during your initial call, you speak directly to the Resolution Officer who will be handling your case.

   b. We need to understand your tax and financial history. The process of gathering all your financial details is often not an easy process, so we work hard to find all the facts we need to effectively represent you.

   c. At the initial meeting, we will discuss possible solutions to your case, and the fees for our services. We do not charge for this initial consultation. If you decide to engage our firm, we will prepare a written agreement of the terms of the engagement, including what we will do for you, and the cost.

   d. Once you sign the retainer agreement, we will prepare a power of attorney form (IRS Form 2848 and 8821) that enables us to speak to the IRS on your behalf. This power of attorney is limited to only representing you before the IRS, and is not a general Power of Attorney for your other affairs, such as estate planning, etc. The Power of Attorney that you sign is revocable by you at any time.

   e. Once you hire us, and sign the Power of Attorney form, we will then immediately file the form 2848 and 8821 with the IRS to show them that we are representing you. This means that all further contact between you and the IRS will be through us, and we will protect your rights. The other strategic benefit of immediately filing the Form 2848 is that when we file a Power of Attorney Form 2848 on your behalf, it is proof to the IRS of your intent to resolve the tax problem quickly. They view this step very favorably in deciding if your case warrants criminal prosecution.

   f. Once we have the authority to represent you, we will take immediate steps to freeze the aggressive actions taken by the IRS so you will not have to worry about the security of your assets while the case is in progress. If tax levies are already in place, we will work with you to have those levies lifted. The steps we take on your behalf will relieve you of stress, and enable you to work with us so we can help you resolve the tax problem.

2. We will request and obtain your MASTER FILE and Transcripts from the IRS that is related to your tax accounts.

   a. We will make sure we have all the tax information the IRS has related to your account so there are no surprises or misunderstandings of your tax issue.

b. The tax data we get from the IRS will assist us in determining the best strategy for us to take to resolve your tax problem.

c. We will use the tax data from the IRS to compare it with the financial account information you provide us with in order to make sure that there is nothing missing from the data we are analyzing.

3. We need to collect financial information from you, and analyze it.

a. This step requires us to obtain accurate financial documents from you in order to see what we can do to improve your situation and reduce your tax liabilities. We also need this information to prepare your tax returns (if needed). We will prepare your tax returns, and will not outsource it to a CPA firm since we find that this only adds unnecessary complexity to your case. We will send you our 'Easy to Use' Tax Organizer documents to help prepare your tax returns.

b. When providing this information, it is important to remember that the tax authorities have the right to question any number on your tax return, so you need the correct guidance from us on what is allowable under the law, and what is not.

c. Once we carefully review all the documentation, we will analyze the situation to see what caused the tax problem in the first place, and how it can be corrected so it does not happen again.

d. We will work together with you to make sure your case is strong, and in your favor. With your cooperation and our professionalism, we guarantee you will have a strong case against the taxing authorities.

4. We will develop an exclusive Resolution strategy to solve your tax problem.

a. After we thoroughly review and discuss your current financial situation with you, we will develop a solution that best suits you. There are a variety of solutions as reviewed in this report. We will discuss each solution with you, and advise you so you can understand the process.

b. Our expertise at negotiating with the IRS will allow you to pay off your debt in a reasonable and timely manner. Every moment you delay taking action to solve your tax problem increases the risk that your situation will get worse. You should not delay -- even if you do not have the money to pay the taxes owed -- since the IRS understands your situation and often allows a tax payment plan that is manageable.

The Services We Offer:

- Remove tax liens
- Remove tax levies
- Stop wage garnishments
- Establish Payments Plan in your best interest
- Representation for audits/exams
- Negotiating Offers in Compromise
- Tax Preparation
- File Back Taxes
- Penalty Abatements

If you know the internal revenue code, IRS policy and believe you are a skilled negotiator, you can possibly work with the IRS yourself. By representing you before the IRS we are able to save you stress, time and money. We know what to say and what not to say and can help you face the IRS without fear. If you don't want to bet your financial future, short or long term on your inexperience with the IRS, call us, we can help. Tax resolution is just a phone call away.

The IRS Tax Helpline guarantees our tax resolution services with a 100% money back guarantee. If we don't provide the resolution service you paid us to perform, we will refund your money 100%, no questions asked.

100% RISK FREE GUARANTEE

To Make You Purchasing Decision Easier, We are Proud to Offer a 60-day Unconditional Money Back Guarantee. If You are Not Completely Satisfied with Your Purchase, Simply Contact Us within 60 Days of Purchase for a Full Refund. No questions asked!

No Worries. No Concerns. Guaranteed!

(Scroll down to view the "Power of Attorney" and Tax Information Authorization forms)

Form **2848** (Rev. March 2012) Department of the Treasury Internal Revenue Service	**Power of Attorney** **and Declaration of Representative** ▶ Type or print. ▶ See the separate instructions.	OMB No. 1545-0150

For IRS Use Only
Received by:
Name _____
Telephone _____
Function _____
Date   /   /

Part I   Power of Attorney

Caution: *A separate Form 2848 should be completed for each taxpayer. Form 2848 will not be honored for any purpose other than representation before the IRS.*

1   Taxpayer information. Taxpayer must sign and date this form on page 2, line 7.

Taxpayer name and address	Taxpayer identification number(s)	
	Daytime telephone number	Plan number (if applicable)

hereby appoints the following representative(s) as attorney(s)-in-fact:

2   Representative(s) must sign and date this form on page 2, Part II.

Name and address	
	CAF No. _____
	PTIN _____
	Telephone No. _____
	Fax No. _____
Check if to be sent notices and communications ☐	Check if new: Address ☐ Telephone No. ☐ Fax No. ☐

Name and address	
	CAF No. _____
	PTIN _____
	Telephone No. _____
	Fax No. _____
Check if to be sent notices and communications ☐	Check if new: Address ☐ Telephone No. ☐ Fax No. ☐

Name and address	
	CAF No. _____
	PTIN _____
	Telephone No. _____
	Fax No. _____
	Check if new: Address ☐ Telephone No. ☐ Fax No. ☐

to represent the taxpayer before the Internal Revenue Service for the following matters:

3   Matters

Description of Matter (Income, Employment, Payroll, Excise, Estate, Gift, Whistleblower, Practitioner Discipline, PLR, FOIA, Civil Penalty, etc.) (see instructions for line 3)	Tax Form Number (1040, 941, 720, etc.) (if applicable)	Year(s) or Period(s) (if applicable) (see instructions for line 3)

4   Specific use not recorded on Centralized Authorization File (CAF). If the power of attorney is for a specific use not recorded on CAF, check this box. See the instructions for Line 4. **Specific Uses Not Recorded on CAF** . . . . ▶ ☐

5   Acts authorized. Unless otherwise provided below, the representatives generally are authorized to receive and inspect confidential tax information and to perform any and all acts that I can perform with respect to the tax matters described on line 3, for example, the authority to sign any agreements, consents, or other documents. The representative(s), however, is (are) not authorized to receive or negotiate any amounts paid to the client in connection with this representation (including refunds by either electronic means or paper checks). Additionally, unless the appropriate box(es) below are checked, the representative(s) is (are) not authorized to execute a request for disclosure of tax returns or return information to a third party, substitute another representative or add additional representatives, or sign certain tax returns.

☐ Disclosure to third parties;   ☐ Substitute or add representative(s);   ☐ Signing a return; _____

☐ Other acts authorized: _____

_____ (see instructions for more information)

Exceptions. An unenrolled return preparer cannot sign any document for a taxpayer and may only represent taxpayers in limited situations. An enrolled actuary may only represent taxpayers to the extent provided in section 10.3(d) of Treasury Department Circular No. 230 (Circular 230). An enrolled retirement plan agent may only represent taxpayers to the extent provided in section 10.3(e) of Circular 230. A registered tax return preparer may only represent taxpayers to the extent provided in section 10.3(f) of Circular 230. See the line 5 instructions for restrictions on tax matters partners. In most cases, the student practitioner's (level k) authority is limited (for example, they may only practice under the supervision of another practitioner).

List any specific deletions to the acts otherwise authorized in this power of attorney: _____

_____

_____

_____

For Privacy Act and Paperwork Reduction Act Notice, see the instructions.   Cat. No. 11980J   Form **2848** (Rev. 3-2012)

Form 2848 (Rev. 3-2012)   Page **2**

6   **Retention/revocation of prior power(s) of attorney.** The filing of this power of attorney automatically revokes all earlier power(s) of attorney on file with the Internal Revenue Service for the same matters and years or periods covered by this document. If you **do not** want to revoke a prior power of attorney, check here . . . . ▶ ☐
YOU MUST ATTACH A COPY OF ANY POWER OF ATTORNEY YOU WANT TO REMAIN IN EFFECT.

7   **Signature of taxpayer.** If a tax matter concerns a year in which a joint return was filed, the husband and wife must each file a separate power of attorney even if the same representative(s) is (are) being appointed. If signed by a corporate officer, partner, guardian, tax matters partner, executor, receiver, administrator, or trustee on behalf of the taxpayer, I certify that I have the authority to execute this form on behalf of the taxpayer.

▶ **IF NOT SIGNED AND DATED, THIS POWER OF ATTORNEY WILL BE RETURNED TO THE TAXPAYER.**

Signature	Date	Title (if applicable)
Print Name	PIN Number ☐☐☐☐☐	Print name of taxpayer from line 1 if other than individual

Part II	**Declaration of Representative**

Under penalties of perjury, I declare that:

- I am not currently under suspension or disbarment from practice before the Internal Revenue Service;
- I am aware of regulations contained in Circular 230 (31 CFR, Part 10), as amended, concerning practice before the Internal Revenue Service;
- I am authorized to represent the taxpayer identified in Part I for the matter(s) specified there; and
- I am one of the following:

  a Attorney—a member in good standing of the bar of the highest court of the jurisdiction shown below.

  b Certified Public Accountant—duly qualified to practice as a certified public accountant in the jurisdiction shown below.

  c Enrolled Agent—enrolled as an agent under the requirements of Circular 230.

  d Officer—a bona fide officer of the taxpayer's organization.

  e Full-Time Employee—a full-time employee of the taxpayer.

  f Family Member—a member of the taxpayer's immediate family (for example, spouse, parent, child, grandparent, grandchild, step-parent, step-child, brother, or sister).

  g Enrolled Actuary—enrolled as an actuary by the Joint Board for the Enrollment of Actuaries under 29 U.S.C. 1242 (the authority to practice before the Internal Revenue Service is limited by section 10.3(d) of Circular 230).

  h Unenrolled Return Preparer—Your authority to practice before the Internal Revenue Service is limited. You must have been eligible to sign the return under examination and have signed the return. **See Notice 2011-6 and Special rules for registered tax return preparers and unenrolled return preparers in the instructions.**

  i Registered Tax Return Preparer—registered as a tax return preparer under the requirements of section 10.4 of Circular 230. Your authority to practice before the Internal Revenue Service is limited. You must have been eligible to sign the return under examination and have signed the return. **See Notice 2011-6 and Special rules for registered tax return preparers and unenrolled return preparers in the instructions.**

  k Student Attorney or CPA—receives permission to practice before the IRS by virtue of his/her status as a law, business, or accounting student working in LITC or STCP under section 10.7(d) of Circular 230. See instructions for Part II for additional information and requirements.

  r Enrolled Retirement Plan Agent—enrolled as a retirement plan agent under the requirements of Circular 230 (the authority to practice before the Internal Revenue Service is limited by section 10.3(e)).

▶ **IF THIS DECLARATION OF REPRESENTATIVE IS NOT SIGNED AND DATED, THE POWER OF ATTORNEY WILL BE RETURNED. REPRESENTATIVES MUST SIGN IN THE ORDER LISTED IN LINE 2 ABOVE.** See the instructions for Part II.

Note: For designations d-f, enter your title, position, or relationship to the taxpayer in the "Licensing jurisdiction" column. See the instructions for Part II for more information.

Designation— Insert above letter (a–r)	Licensing jurisdiction (state) or other licensing authority (if applicable)	Bar, license, certification, registration, or enrollment number (if applicable). See instructions for Part II for more information.	Signature	Date

Form **2848** (Rev. 3-2012)

Form **8821**

(Rev. October 2011)

Department of the Treasury
Internal Revenue Service

Tax Information Authorization

▶ Do not sign this form unless all applicable lines have been completed.
▶ Do not use this form to request a copy or transcript of your tax return.
Instead, use Form 4506 or Form 4506-T.

OMB No. 1545-1165

For IRS Use Only

Received by:
Name _____
Telephone _____
Function _____
Date _____

---

1 Taxpayer information. Taxpayer(s) must sign and date this form on line 7.

Taxpayer name(s) and address (type or print)	Taxpayer identification number
	Daytime telephone number	Plan number (if applicable)

---

2 Appointee. If you wish to name more than one appointee, attach a list to this form.

Name and address	CAF No.
	PTIN
	Telephone No.
	Fax No.
	Check if new: Address ☐ Telephone No. ☐ Fax No. ☐

---

3 Tax matters. The appointee is authorized to inspect and/or receive confidential tax information in any office of the IRS for the tax matters listed on this line. Do not use Form 8821 to request copies of tax returns.

(a) Type of Tax (Income, Employment, Excise, etc.) or Civil Penalty	(b) Tax Form Number (1040, 941, 720, etc.)	(c) Year(s) or Period(s) (see the instructions for line 3)	(d) Specific Tax Matters (see instr.)

---

4 Specific use not recorded on Centralized Authorization File (CAF). If the tax information authorization is for a specific use not recorded on CAF, check this box. See the instructions on page 4. If you check this box, skip lines 5 and 6 . . ▶ ☐

---

5 Disclosure of tax information (you **must** check a box on line 5a or 5b unless the box on line 4 is checked):

a If you want copies of tax information, notices, and other written communications sent to the appointee on an ongoing basis, check this box . . . . ▶ ☐

Note. Appointees will no longer receive forms, publications and other related materials with the notices.

b If you do not want any copies of notices or communications sent to your appointee, check this box . . . . ▶ ☐

---

6 Retention/revocation of tax information authorizations. This tax information authorization automatically revokes all prior authorizations for the same tax matters you listed on line 3 above unless you checked the box on line 4. If you do not want to revoke a prior tax information authorization, you **must** attach a copy of any authorizations you want to remain in effect and check this box . . . . ▶ ☐

To revoke this tax information authorization, see the instructions on page 4.

---

7 Signature of taxpayer(s). If a tax matter applies to a joint return, **either** husband or wife must sign. If signed by a corporate officer, partner, guardian, executor, receiver, administrator, trustee, or party other than the taxpayer, I certify that I have the authority to execute this form with respect to the tax matters/periods on line 3 above.

▶ **IF NOT SIGNED AND DATED, THIS TAX INFORMATION AUTHORIZATION WILL BE RETURNED.**

▶ **DO NOT SIGN THIS FORM IF IT IS BLANK OR INCOMPLETE.**

Signature	Date	Signature	Date
Print Name	Title (if applicable)	Print Name	Title (if applicable)
☐ ☐ ☐ ☐ ☐ PIN number for electronic signature		☐ ☐ ☐ ☐ ☐ PIN number for electronic signature	

For Privacy Act and Paperwork Reduction Act Notice, see page 4.   Cat. No. 11596P   Form **8821** (Rev. 10-2011)

LEGAL NOTICE

The IRS Tax Helpline is a division of EurAsia Financial Inc. and is not affiliated with the United States Internal Revenue Service. In conjunction with our website www.irstaxhelpline.com we strive to be as accurate and complete as possible in the creation of this report, notwithstanding the fact that we do not warrant or represent at any time that the contents within are accurate due to the rapidly changing nature of the IRS and other government forces and conditions.

While all attempts have been made to verify information provided in this publication, we assume no responsibility for errors, omissions, or contrary interpretation of the subject matter herein. Any perceived slights of specific persons, peoples, or organizations are unintentional.

In practical advice books, like anything else in life, there are no guarantees. Readers are cautioned to rely on their own judgment about their individual circumstances to act accordingly.

This report is not intended for use as a source of legal, business, accounting or financial advice. All readers are advised to seek services of competent professionals in legal, business, accounting, and finance field.

Client understands that results with the IRS are neither promised nor guaranteed. Client understands that Company has made no warranties or guarantees relating to its Services. Company's promises contained herein are to use its best efforts to complete the Services as detailed in this report. Company is paid for its efforts and not for results. Company fully relies on the information obtained from both the IRS and the Client to complete the Services detailed herein. Client's obligation to pay Company are not determined by results or relief obtained.

The Privacy Policy of the Company is to 'Not Disclose' any information obtained by the Client to any non affiliated third party not involved in the execution of the Services provided in our Agreement.

You are encouraged to print this report for easy reading and future reference.

Would you like a free consultation?

You can call now for your free consultation or visit us on line either desktop or on your mobile device at
www.irstaxhelpline.com

Unlike _all_ other companies, there is no minimum amount of taxes you owe the IRS for us to help you with.

Please take a few moments to view our video at
www.irstaxhelpline.com

So call us today at 1-855-240-1040

Thank you for reading our eBook. We hope we have helped you to better understand how you can overcome your IRS problems.

Please feel free to contact us with any questions, additional information or help that you may need.

Jules Marcel